E-mail
Success!

S0-CFE-368

Professional
Style

Visual
Impact

Reader
Focus

Business
Judgment

Simple Steps to E-mail Success

Joy Van Skiver
author of

The Writing Exchange
Business Style Guide

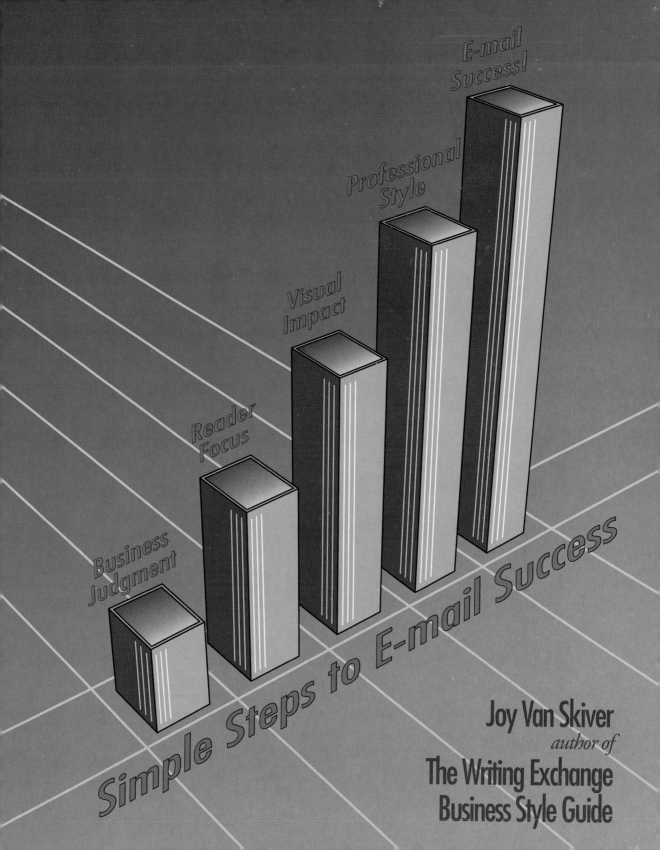

Simple Steps to E-mail Success
Copyright © 1999 by The Writing Exchange, Inc.

Published by WREXpress
A Division of The Writing Exchange, Inc.
466 Southern Boulevard
Chatham, New Jersey 07928
Telephone: (973) 822-8400
Facsimile: (973) 822-8411
E-mail: WritingEx@aol.com

Library of Congress Cataloging-in-Publication Data

Van Skiver, Joy, 1947–
    Simple steps to e-mail success / Joy Van Skiver.
        p.   cm.
    ISBN 0-9643824-2-3 (pbk.)
    1. Electronic mail systems.   I. Title.
    HE7551.V36 1998
    004.692—dc21   98-54122
                                           CIP

Printed and bound in The United States of America.

Simple Steps to E-mail Success can be ordered at special discounts for distribution within organizations. If you prefer, WREXpress can create a customized edition with your corporate name and logo, and perhaps an introductory message from your CEO. Licenses are also available to print unlimited copies for internal use.

To Burt,
my husband and business partner.

E-mail is here to stay! It's easy. It's convenient. It's cheap. It's fast. And it's fun.

As a business writing consultant for over 20 years, I've watched e-mail grow from a crude tool used by a few "techies" to a technological marvel that provides instantaneous communication for virtually everyone with a computer.

Everyone learns the mechanical side of e-mail in a snap. *Hit this key to ...* is as simple as a basic cookbook. But there's also a thinking side to e-mail, and that's what this book is all about.

Along the way, I've answered hundreds of questions about the structure and style of e-mail messages. I've heard lots of complaints about e-mail, too, particularly that it eats up valuable time. However, that's not the only issue confronting us.

Business e-mail is under a microscope right now because of its legal ramifications. Messages that were written in haste have shown up in lawsuits receiving worldwide news coverage. As a result, major corporations are examining e-mail policies and encouraging employees to watch what they say. One organization has even installed a monitoring device that tags words that could cause trouble down the road.

Unlike personal e-mail messages at home where "anything goes," business e-mail needs guidelines. Without them, we will waste the advantages of the greatest business invention since the desktop computer.

When was the last time you read a 62-page business book? Like a good e-mail message, *Simple Steps* does not require a lot of your time. It's certainly not something you need to study! Just read it, "climb" the steps, and reap the benefits!

Joy Van Skiver

February 1999

Contents

Business Judgment **1**

    E-mail Overload 3
    Liability 4
    Response Time 5
    Proactive Communication 5
    Chain Mail 5
    Privacy 6
    Just the Facts 6
    Attachments 7
    Walking to Talk 8
    Social Announcements 8
    Meaningless Tricks 9
    Pass the Word 9

Reader Focus **11**

    Time and Action Up Front 13
    Bottom Line vs. Stream of Consciousness 17
    Specific Subject Lines 18
    First Line Success 19

Visual Impact **21**

    Stop SHOUTING 23
    Headings and White Space 24
    Your Reader's Screen 25
    Lists 26

Professional Style **29**

    Personalized Messages 31
    Repeating a Sender's Message 31
    Emoticons and E-mail Jargon 32
    Flaming 33
    Signature Files 33
    Talking vs. Announcing 34
    Typos 34
    Cultural Differences 35
    Positive vs. Negative 36
    Sentence Length 36
    Paragraphs 37
    Readability with Numbers 38
    Run-on Sentences 40
    Repetition 41

Contents

E-mail Success **43**

Business Judgment 46
Reader Focus 47
Visual Impact 48
Professional Style 49

The Writing Exchange **53**

Business Writing Specialists since 1978 55
Coaching by Mail 56
The Writing Exchange Business Style Guide 57
Selling on Paper – The Way to Write to Customers 58
Reminders from The Writing Exchange 59
Order Form 60
About the Author 61
Colophon 62

Business
Judgment

Reader
Focus

Visual
Impact

Professional
Style

E-mail
Success!

Simple Steps to E-mail Success

The business world has always had rules—many of them unspoken and not documented—but everyone comes to know what's acceptable and what's not. Be sure to stay on top of expectations, priorities and protocol within your organization. It's so easy to use e-mail, but your computer is not equipped with a Good Judgment key. Business decisions are still up to you.

Always make decisions based on (1) your reader and (2) the content of your message. Considering these two factors will help you choose how much detail to include, when to send copies to others, and when to use special e-mail features. You may even decide to use another means of communicating altogether.

E-mail Overload

Before you send copies of your message to a number of people, think about their e-mail load. Are your colleagues receiving hundreds of messages a day? If you gain a reputation for including people who don't need your messages, they may start deleting your messages without even reading them!

When you're concerned about keeping everyone informed and you have a long cc list, add a note at the end of your message to give people a choice:

Unless your organization's policy specifically dictates otherwise, most messages do not merit "telling the world." To help you decide when a Send All is appropriate, consider old-fashioned inter-office mail.

> Carl, a programmer analyst in a department of 125 people, sent a message that he would be out of the office for a few days. He had good intentions, but he sent it to everyone. Most of them didn't even know Carl. Would he have made the same decision if his method of communicating had been a memo in the inter-office mail?

Liability

Since e-mail messages can be used in lawsuits, consider the risk before you say something that could work against you or your organization. Did you know that even deleted messages can be retrieved years later?

Three years ago, Satish in Quality Assurance and Ryan in Marketing had an e-mail conversation about SafetyOpen, a new product being released. Satish told Ryan:

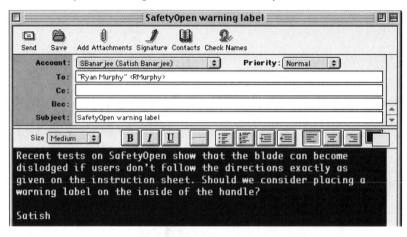

Ryan's return message said:

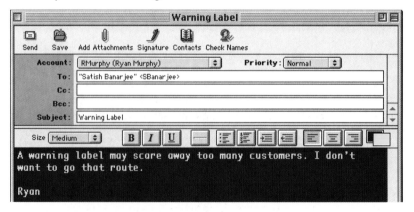

Now, as part of a class action suit, lawyers for the plaintiffs have requested electronic retrieval of any message related to SafetyOpen. Would you like to guess who's going to win this one and what the settlement is likely to be?

Response Time

The instant nature of e-mail creates the illusion that as soon as you send a message the receiver reads it. Your expectations for a quick response may be especially high when you tag your message as urgent.

What is considered a reasonable response time in your company's culture? A good rule of thumb is to post at least some response, if not a complete one, within one business day.

When you know someone is expecting a reply but you must delay, you can use a short "what's happening" message such as the following:

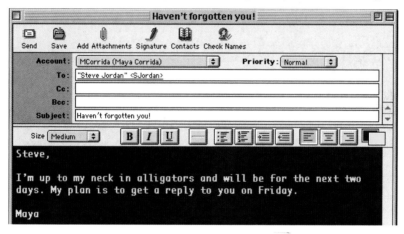

These simple messages don't require a lot of time, and you will enhance your image by responding promptly.

Proactive Communication

Choose some method of managing your mail when you're away. An auto response, for example, will send a reply such as, "I'll be on vacation until November 17," to anyone who sends you a message.

Another option is to ask someone to read your mail and respond for you. You can auto forward your mail to this person or set up a temporary password that this individual can use.

Your proactive communication can keep business operations moving smoothly and save you a few "headaches" when you return.

Chain Mail

When someone sends you a message and copies in five people, do you respond with copies to the same people? Why? Because it's a simple keystroke? It's quite possible that the five copyholders needed to know the first message but not the second. You could continue the chain or you could choose to stop it.

Privacy

Although it's improbable that systems administrators or hackers are looking at your mail, it *is* possible. Remember also, that employers own their e-mail systems; they can legally inspect anyone's mail.

To be safe, think of e-mail messages as conversations you're having in an open area. When you need to discuss sensitive situations or communicate information you don't want others to know about, use the phone or set up a face-to-face meeting.

Be extremely careful not to send a confidential message to the wrong people.

> Andrea wishes she had met with Denitia instead of sending an e-mail message. She accidentally selected Department Distribution (right below Denitia in her address book) instead of highlighting Denitia, then she hit Send. Before Andrea realized what had happened, everyone found out about Denitia's unprofessional manner at a recent convention. By then it was too late to hit Unsend.

Just the Facts

When you communicate in person, people are influenced 55% by your nonverbals (facial expressions, eye contact and body language), 38% by your tone of voice, and only 7% by the actual words you use. These statistics are based on a well-known study by Albert Mehrabian, Ph.D., Professor of Psychology at U.C.L.A.

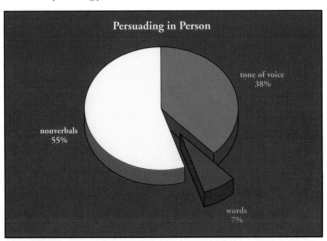

When you communicate by e-mail, you must rely totally on words. What's worth 7% in person becomes 100% on a screen. Since humor and irony are extremely difficult to convey in words, why take the chance that someone might misinterpret you? Stick to the facts and just the facts.

Attachments

Most systems allow you to "attach" documents to your message. Before you do that, ask yourself, "Will this attachment help my reader?" Sending an attachment may be easy for you, but reading it may be time consuming for the receiver. If your reader doesn't need an entire spreadsheet, for example, put only the required numbers in your e-mail message instead of attaching the spreadsheet.

Sometimes your reader's system may not be able to handle your attachment's file format or size. If you're not sure, ask your systems administrator. You may have to take special steps to avoid problems.

Remember that downloading attachments takes time. While they may know how large an attachment is, receivers have no way of knowing how valuable it is for them before they download it. Will they be annoyed when they finally read the attachment, only to discover it was something they didn't need?

Old-fashioned memos often had attachments, but readers could take a 5-second glance at the hard copy to determine its value. Until e-mail can provide something similar, it's wise to think twice before attaching documents.

A smart choice, especially when you have more than one attachment, is to let your readers know exactly what they'll find in the attachments.

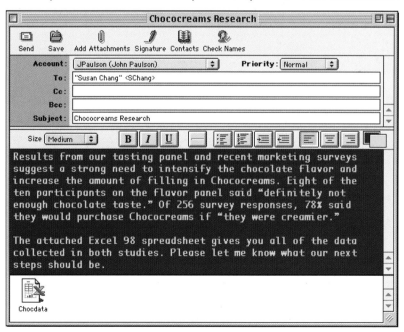

Walking to Talk

Does anyone talk face-to-face any more? E-mail has become so automatic that people forget they have other options. Here's a case in point:

> Marion's cubicle is about eight feet from Chad's. At least twice a week, she sends him a short e-mail that she could easily deliver in person. Since no one is getting copies of the message, it's logical to do that. A message that takes five minutes for Marion to type and five minutes for Chad to open and read may take a total of only two minutes in person.

Social Announcements

E-mail has opened a Pandora's box when it comes to social announcements. Since literally everyone in an organization can receive e-mail, no one has to miss the news about retirements, promotions, company picnics and other social occasions.

In the "old days," paper notices were thumb-tacked on hallway bulletin boards, announcements appeared in newsletters, and desk drops informed everyone in the building. Now that people think globally, they may forget that most social events are local. Why impose on someone to open and read an announcement that does not affect him or her?

Consider the following situation:

> When Sal in Engineering decided to retire, Hudson sent global e-mail to all 1500 people in the company. Only about 20 people had ever worked with Sal. Ten of those people sent "Congratulations" and "Best Wishes" messages to Sal and copied in all 1500 people. How much time was wasted just because Hudson found it easier to do a Send All than to pinpoint the people who knew Sal?

Staff members who work in the field usually say they receive too much mail from their corporate headquarters. The more e-mail they receive that's irrelevant to them, the more likely they will ignore messages from those same departments.

Here's a typical example:

> At the corporate headquarters of a large organization, Reva in Human Resources sent a message inviting everyone to a reception from 6:00 to 7:00 P.M. honoring a new executive vice president. For the 750 employees at the corporate headquarters, it was feasible for them to attend. For the 3000 employees scattered throughout the country, the message was ludicrous.

Meaningless Tricks

What percentage of your messages are marked *Urgent*? Do they merit that classification, or is this just a way to trick someone into reading the message?

Urgent is used so often that it has lost its significance. Instead of relying on meaningless tricks to motivate your reader, focus on the content and form of your message. When you consistently show that your messages are valuable, people will read them.

Pass the Word

If e-mail is eating up too much of your time, start talking about it at team meetings, business lunches and casual conversations with colleagues. Change will occur only when people pass the word!

Business Judgment

Reader Focus

Visual Impact

Professional Style

E-mail Success!

Simple Steps to E-mail Success

People pay attention to messages that involve them. Remember that everyone reads with the viewpoint of "What's in it for me?"

To get maximum results from your e-mail messages, take 30 seconds to think about your reader before you begin to type. Three questions will help you focus on the person or people receiving your message:

- What does my reader need?
- What do I want my reader to do?
- Why am I sending this message?

Time and Action Up Front

Have you ever missed a deadline or a meeting because you skimmed an e-mail message and didn't see a date? Be sure you put deadlines and meeting dates in the first three lines. Which of these e-mail messages would you rather receive?

Cancellations

Send Save Add Attachments Signature Contacts Check Names

Account: SMasters (Skye Masters)   Priority: Normal
To: "Maria Alonzo" <MAlonzo>
Cc:
Bcc:
Subject: Cancellations

Size Medium   B I U

I would like to follow up on our conversation about cancellations and fill you in on the results of our examination of the renewal process. Both of these topics may come up at tomorrow's meeting, so I want to inform you prior to the meeting.

Is it possible to get together this afternoon at 2:00 or after? If so, I'll come up to your office.

Cancellations

Send Save Add Attachments Signature Contacts Check Names

Account: SMasters (Skye Masters)   Priority: Normal
To: "Maria Alonzo" <MAlonzo>
Cc:
Bcc:
Subject: Cancellations

Size Medium   B I U

Can we get together this afternoon to discuss two topics that may come up at tomorrow's meeting? I would like to tell you more about cancellations and fill you in on our examination of the renewal process.

Will 2:00 or later work for you? If so, I'll come up to your office.

13

Put requests for information or action in the beginning of your message. Sometimes you can use a direct question, just as you would in person.

In the following message, the sender's question doesn't appear until the eighth line:

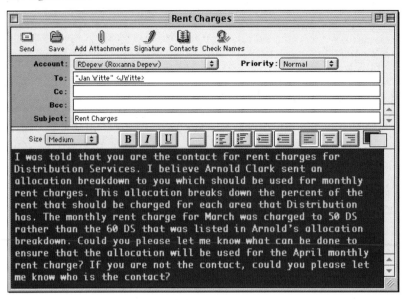

Note how the up-front request and numbered, direct questions make this message easier to read:

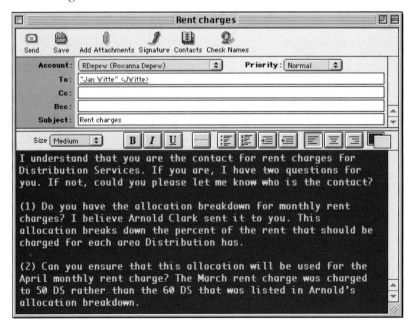

When you need to give a direction, put it up front. People appreciate knowing what you want from them before you go into a lot of details.

When Don starts reading the following message, will he care about what happened last month?

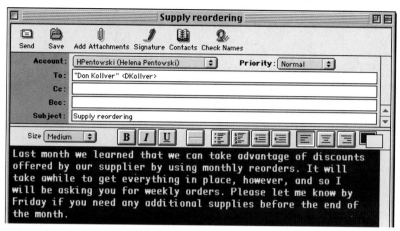

Don could read just the first sentence of the following message and decide what action he needs to take:

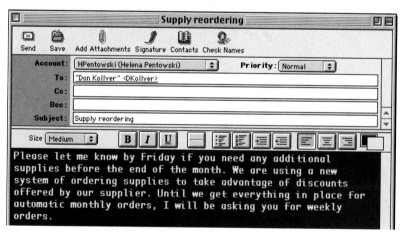

If you want to be careful of tone in your direction, begin your message with a reason for the request or a benefit for the reader. Also use the words *you* and *yours*.

Here's a message that probably will not capture the reader's attention:

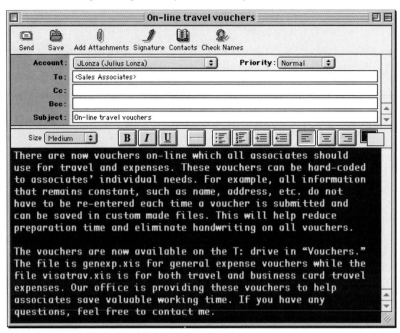

Note in this revision that the benefit is up front, the word *you* appears five times and *yours* appears twice:

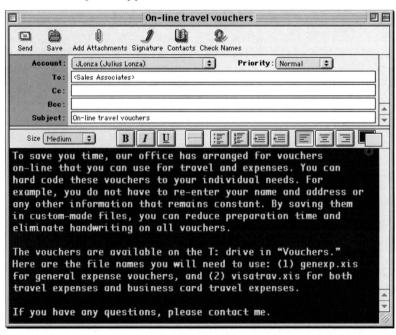

Bottom Line vs. Stream of Consciousness

Most complaints about the content of e-mail have to do with lengthy messages that don't get to the point. Because writers tend to write as they think, their messages may follow a chronological approach. They end up telling a story and wasting the reader's time.

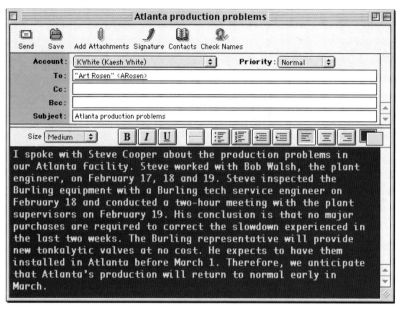

Go ahead and write your message the way you think it. Then, take an extra minute to move your bottom line message to the top. Art doesn't have to read all of the following message to know what's important:

Specific Subject Lines

Like a memo, an e-mail message needs a subject or reference line to help your reader quickly identify why you're communicating. Make your subject line as specific as you can without creating a complete sentence. To avoid boring your reader, don't use the very same wording as the first line of your message.

Here's a line that gets Keeshawn's reader involved immediately:

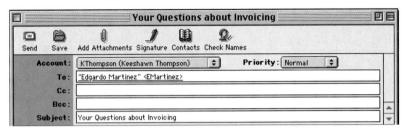

Although no one likes to hear bad news, a line announcing problems can be very effective when the people receiving the message are the ones responsible for the solutions.

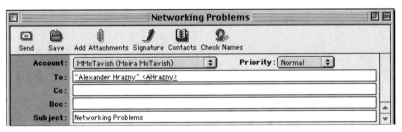

A specific date can motivate Robert's reader to check the message for details about time and place.

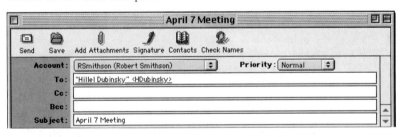

First Line Success

You're more likely to get your reader's attention if the first sentence of your message:

- Has no more than 20 words.

- Includes *you* or *your*.

When Nancy reads the following message, she will probably be put off by the 47-word opening sentence and the references to *I, her* and *she*:

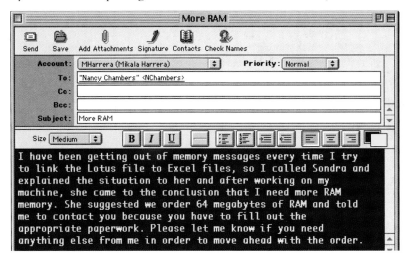

Here's a message that captures Nancy's attention:

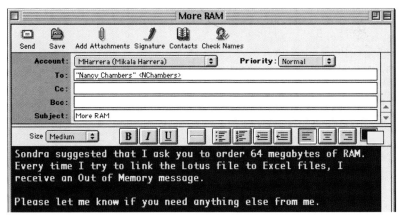

Business
Judgment

Reader
Focus

Visual
Impact

Professional
Style

E-mail
Success!

Simple Steps to E-mail Success

When you pay attention to the appearance of your messages, people spend less time reading them and more time acting on them.

Stop SHOUTING

Have you seen e-mail messages entirely in upper case letters? In the world of e-mail, this is considered shouting. Usually, shouting occurs because the writer hits the Caps Lock key to avoid the extra effort of hitting the Shift key periodically. Since readability studies have proven it takes longer to read an all upper case message, it makes sense to use upper and lower case.

Which of these two messages is easier to read?

Always use capital letters to start sentences, to distinguish proper names, and to use the word *I* correctly. Messages written entirely in lower case are just as difficult to read as all caps.

Headings and White Space

Until technological improvements become available on all systems, rely on headings and white space to enhance the format of your message:

- Leave a space between paragraphs to give your reader some breathing room.

- Divide long paragraphs (more than 10 lines of type) into shorter ones (3 to 6 lines) to encourage your reader to keep reading.

- Use headings in all caps or bold to help you create separate sections in a longer message. Because most business readers want to skim messages, headings can make that easy for them.

  Headings can also help you organize your thoughts. When you're ready to write a long message, think of headings first. Type the headings, then fill in the information you need below the headings.

  Make sure you have at least two headings; just one does not make sense. Also, avoid using Roman numerals or letters next to headings. The words by themselves will stand out for your reader.

Hildie will probably be confused after reading this message:

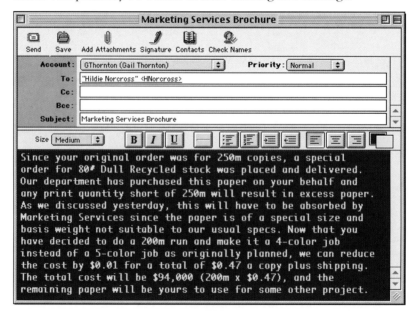

Hildie can easily skim this message and focus on the numbers she needs:

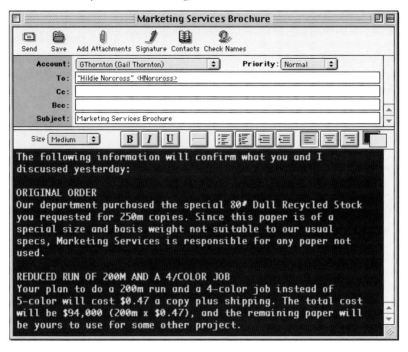

Your Reader's Screen

When you're communicating within your own organization on one system, what you see on your screen is what your reader will see. Some systems, however, do not recognize tabs, bullets, bold, italics, "curly" quotes, or other special characters. When in doubt about these characters, leave them out.

Lists

When used appropriately, lists can help your reader move quickly through your message. Used illogically or presented haphazardly, however, they can cause your reader to stumble.

When a list completes a thought begun in an introductory sentence, start each listed item with the same word form. Frequently, you will be using verbs to do this.

Note how the list in the following example accents the three actions Chris will take:

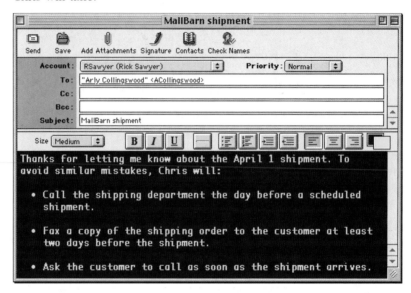

If your system allows it and your reader's system permits it, indent vertical lists about a half inch to an inch from the left margin. The extra "white space" will draw your reader's eyes to this section of your message.

If you can, be sure to use "hanging indents" to align the text so that there is no text underneath a bullet.

Horizontal lists can be effective when you want to stress three or four short points in a single sentence. Use numbers in parentheses to accent each item.

This 20-word sentence does not need to have a vertical list:

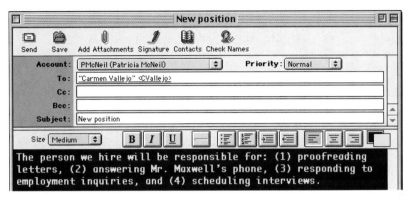

If you are using just five or six words in your entire list, numbers are not necessary.

In the following example, the first part of the short sentence makes it clear there are three systems:

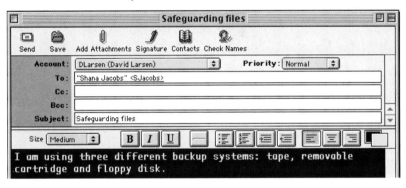

Business
Judgment

Reader
Focus

Visual
Impact

Professional
Style

E-mail
Success!

Simple Steps to E-mail Success

Your e-mail correspondence says a lot about you. Just as with any other form of business communication, messages on the screen give others an opportunity to observe your style.

Personalized Messages

If you want to personalize the beginning of a message you're sending to one reader, use the person's name in direct address as you would in person. Don't use formal salutations (*Dear ...*) or closings (*Sincerely*) as you do in letters.

If you're making a request and want to end by expressing your appreciation, use the word *Thanks* followed by your name. Use the word *Regards* for messages you send internationally.

The following message is direct and business-friendly:

```
┌──────────────────────── Sales figures ────────────────────────┐
│  ⬚    ⬚      ⬚          ✎         📖        👤                  │
│ Send  Save  Add Attachments  Signature  Contacts  Check Names  │
│   Account: │ CConnors (Carole Connors)    ⬍ │  Priority: Normal ⬍│
│        To: │ "Hans Vanderveld" <HVanderveld>                    │
│        Cc: │                                                    │
│       Bcc: │                                                    │
│   Subject: │ Sales figures                                      │
├────────────────────────────────────────────────────────────────┤
│  Size │Medium ⬍│   B  I  U  │ — │ ▤ ▤ ▤ ▤ │ ▤ ▤ ▤ │ ◻          │
├────────────────────────────────────────────────────────────────┤
│ Hans,                                                           │
│                                                                 │
│ Can you send me the sales figures for the thermographic         │
│ products? I'd like to discuss them with Murray on Friday.       │
│                                                                 │
│ Thanks,                                                         │
│ Carole                                                          │
└────────────────────────────────────────────────────────────────┘
```

Ending a message with just your name also adds a personal touch.

When you're sending a message to a number of people, avoid phony greetings such as *Hi Folks* or *Hi Everyone*. Would you start a memo that way? Simply begin with your message. That's always an acceptable style for business.

Repeating a Sender's Message

Most systems allow you to include the sender's entire message in your reply. If that message is lengthy, however, your reader may prefer just a line or two as a reminder.

If your system doesn't automatically place the sender's message below yours, move it to the end of your reply. In most cases, your reader wants to see your reply first.

Think of a repeat of the sender's message as optional information that some people may need but others will not.

Emoticons and E-mail Jargon

If you have traveled on the information superhighway, you've probably seen symbols created from punctuation marks. These are known as emoticons or smileys. Since most business professionals do not want or need cute symbols, reserve them for personal e-mail messages.

E-mail jargon, in the form of acronyms, has also become popular on the Net. If you know your readers understand and appreciate the inside lingo, an acronym such as *FWIW* (*for what it's worth*) or *BTW* (*by the way*) will not jeopardize your professional image. If your readers are not familiar with an acronym, however, they will waste time trying to figure it out. In most cases, you can simply eliminate the jargon.

Elise may "get" the emoticons here, but will she understand the jargon?

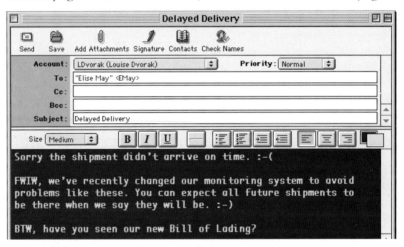

This message doesn't require any guessing:

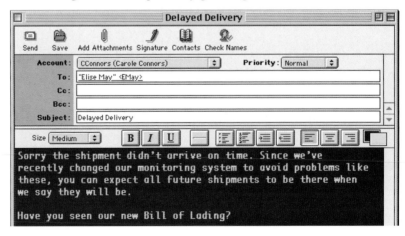

Flaming

The instant nature of e-mail makes it easy to send emotionally charged messages without stopping to think about the consequences. Flaming is the term that has developed to define incendiary messages on e-mail.

If you're angry or annoyed when you are writing an e-mail message, walk away from your computer for a moment. Before you send the message, ask yourself, "Will this message cause more trouble than I want?"

Getting caught in a flame war is usually not productive.

If you must communicate a stern message by e-mail, choose your words carefully. Avoid using all caps, underlining, bold face or exclamation marks to make your point.

Here's an example of a message that probably will not be well received:

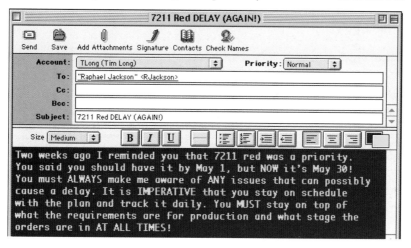

Signature Files

Signature files that automatically end your messages with your name and phone number can be very practical. If you include in that file a famous quote or a motivational saying or drawing, keep in mind that every message will end with it. Since it may not appear on your screen, you could forget you're sending it with every message. What's clever to you might annoy someone else.

Talking vs. Announcing

When you're sending a message to several people, think of talking to one person at a time. You are not making a speech from a podium, and people are not together in one group as they read your message.

Avoid third person terms such as *employees, associates* and *they*. Use *you* when it's logical.

Note how the following message sounds like an announcement:

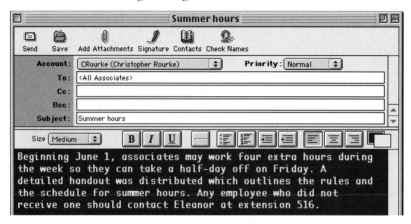

This sounds like one human being talking to one other human being:

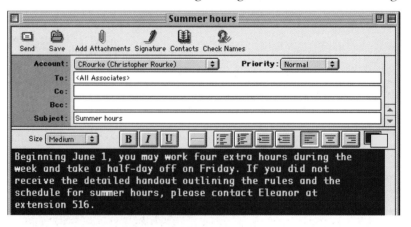

Typos

Every human being makes mistakes when typing quickly. People who don't take an extra minute or two to correct their mistakes, however, risk being perceived as sloppy, lazy or incompetent.

Why put your credibility on the line? At the very least, set up a default that runs your spellchecker when you hit Send. Although spellcheckers don't catch everything, they can correct many typos and word errors.

Cultural Differences

In most cases it's quite acceptable to write very direct e-mail messages. Be aware, however, that some cultures perceive a direct style as too pushy. If you offend your reader, you may not get the results you want.

For many people, the following message sounds demanding despite the use of *please* and *thank you*:

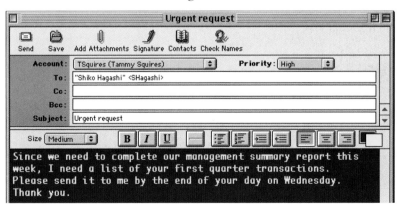

When you're concerned about being too direct, try giving a reason for a request. The tone is usually less demanding. Also avoid any wording that suggests you expect people to drop everything and do what you want. Using conversational words such as *you, your, our, me, my, us* and *I* always contribute to a friendly style.

Note how the tone of this message sounds collaborative:

To avoid confusion in international e-mail, don't use numbers and slashes to express dates. To Americans, 7/4/98 is July 4, 1998. In other countries, however, it means April 7, 1998.

Positive vs. Negative

Emphasize what you *can* do for your reader rather than what you *cannot* do. When you put a positive spin on the news, your readers are more likely to stay tuned. Look for words such as *not, no, none* and *never.* Try to reword your message to use positive words instead.

The following message sounds like the writer is annoyed with the reader:

This message makes the reader feel like she's getting what she wants:

Sentence Length

A major cause of confusion in e-mail messages is the use of long sentences. To make sure you're clear, keep your average sentence length in the range of 14 to 20 words.

If you have to use long sentences, try to balance them by using short sentences close by. This is especially important if you are communicating technical information to a nontechnical reader.

Keep in mind that the shorter the sentence, the greater the emphasis. That's true as long as all of your sentences are not too short. If your average sentence length is below 10, for example, there may not be an opportunity for any one sentence to stand out.

Paragraphs

Don't throw away good paragraph structure in an effort to simplify messages. A screen full of one- or two-line thoughts can actually appear to be unorganized.

Five very short paragraphs make this message seem to be several separate ideas:

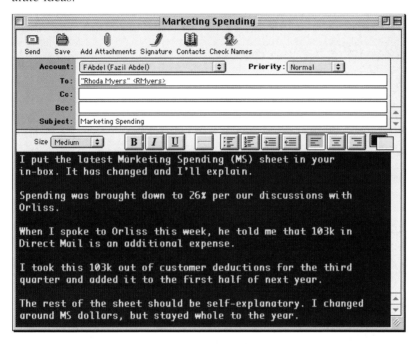

Here, Rhoda gets the impression that the writer is organized:

Readability with Numbers

To lower the risk of confusion, avoid more than four numbers in one sentence. If necessary, break a sentence into two or three separate ones. Also, avoid taking your reader through a calculation from beginning to end; start with the final number and then go back through the calculation.

The following message may confuse Pierre:

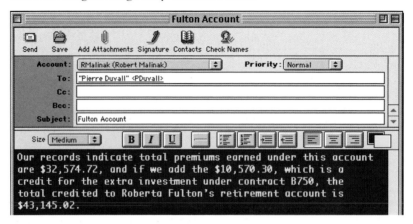

Note how much clearer the message can be:

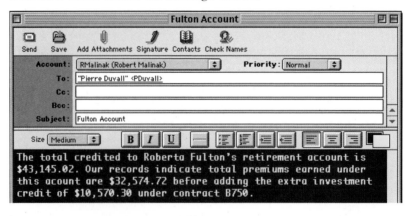

When the numbers you're using are dates, time of day or other non-dollar numbers, use headings and lists to help your reader follow the details. Having the month as a word instead of a number can improve readability.

Gavin will have trouble deciphering this message:

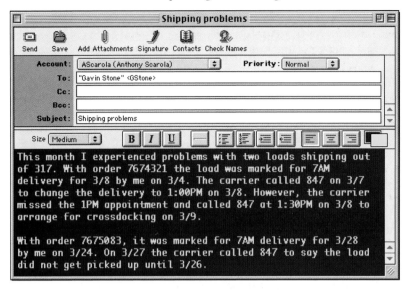

This revision is perfectly clear:

Shipping problems

Send   Save   Add Attachments Signature Contacts Check Names

Account: AScarola (Anthony Scarola)   **Priority:** Normal
To: "Gavin Stone" <GStone>
Cc:
Bcc:
Subject: Shipping problems

Size Medium   B I U

```
This month I experienced problems with two loads shipping out
of 317.

Order 7674321
March 4   I marked the load for 7AM delivery on March 8.
March 7   The carrier called 847 to change the delivery to 1PM
          on March 8.
March 8   The carrier missed the 1PM appointment and called
          847 at 1:30PM to arrange for crossdocking on March 9.

Order 7675083
March 24 I marked the load for 7AM delivery on March 28.
March 27 The carrier called 847 to say the load did not get
          picked up until March 26.
```

Run-on Sentences

Run-on sentences are not just long sentences. They are mistakes caused by combining two complete thoughts incorrectly. When you make this mistake, your reader may think you're rambling or that you're careless.

Although you might *create* a message with run-ons because you're in a hurry, you can *fix it before you send it.* Taking thirty seconds to insert a few periods could save your reader's time to decipher your message, save your time to clarify what you meant, and protect your professional image.

This message sounds like the writer is rambling:

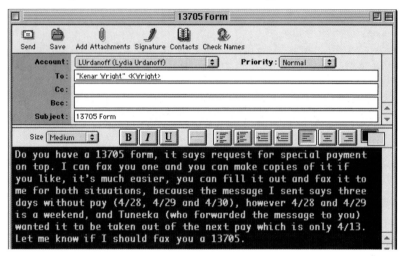

Note how punctuation can change "verbal spaghetti" into an orderly, organized message.

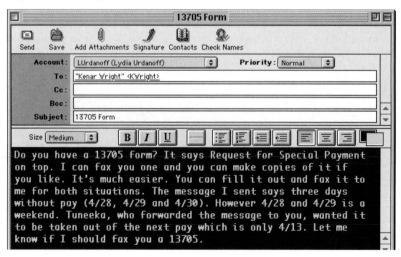

Repetition

When your messages are wordy, people don't read them. Before you hit Send, check for repetition that you can easily cut. Keep in mind that headings and lists can help you say something once instead of twice.

Here's a message that the writer didn't edit:

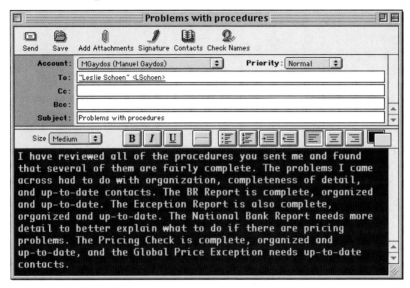

Contrast that message with this clear, concise one:

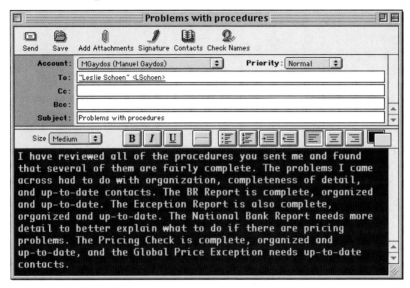

Business
Judgment

Reader
Focus

Visual
Impact

Professional
Style

E-mail
Success!

Simple Steps to E-mail Success

When you make smart decisions about e-mail, you will:

- Receive responses to your questions and requests without having to follow up by phone or with another e-mail message.

- Avoid negative reactions, liability issues and interpersonal conflicts.

- Gain a reputation for communicating effectively.

- Contribute to the overall efficiency and productivity of your organization.

The 16 Help Screens in this chapter will remind you how Simple it is to climb the Steps to E-mail Success.

Your computer is not equipped with a Good Judgment key. Business decisions are still up to you. Stay on top of documented policy as well as the unwritten rules in your organization, and make a concerted effort to change ineffective e-mail habits in your business area.

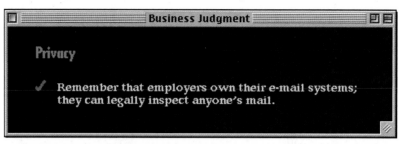

Business Judgment

Privacy

✓ Remember that employers own their e-mail systems; they can legally inspect anyone's mail.

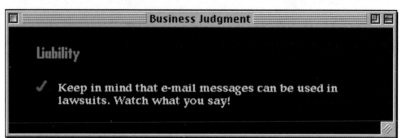

Business Judgment

Liability

✓ Keep in mind that e-mail messages can be used in lawsuits. Watch what you say!

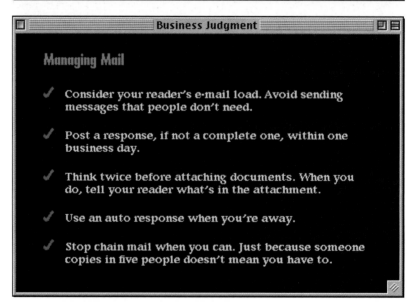

Business Judgment

Managing Mail

✓ Consider your reader's e-mail load. Avoid sending messages that people don't need.

✓ Post a response, if not a complete one, within one business day.

✓ Think twice before attaching documents. When you do, tell your reader what's in the attachment.

✓ Use an auto response when you're away.

✓ Stop chain mail when you can. Just because someone copies in five people doesn't mean you have to.

Everyone reads with the viewpoint of "What's in it for me?" By thinking about your reader before you begin to type, you will create reader-
focused messages that capture attention.

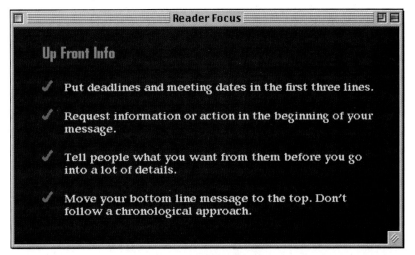

Up Front Info

✓ Put deadlines and meeting dates in the first three lines.

✓ Request information or action in the beginning of your
message.

✓ Tell people what you want from them before you go
into a lot of details.

✓ Move your bottom line message to the top. Don't
follow a chronological approach.

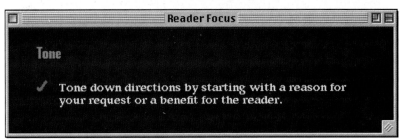

Tone

✓ Tone down directions by starting with a reason for
your request or a benefit for the reader.

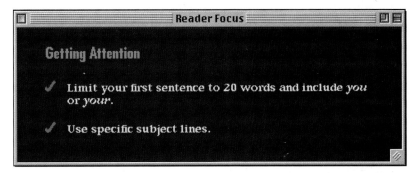

Getting Attention

✓ Limit your first sentence to 20 words and include *you*
or *your*.

✓ Use specific subject lines.

The appearance of your message influences your reader's willingness to read it. People ignore or delay acting on messages that look complex. Visually appealing messages get read!

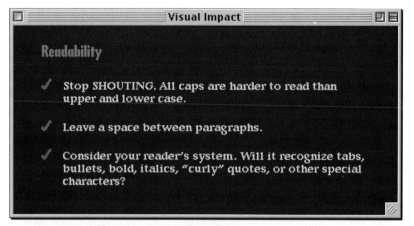

Visual Impact

Readability

✓ Stop SHOUTING. All caps are harder to read than upper and lower case.

✓ Leave a space between paragraphs.

✓ Consider your reader's system. Will it recognize tabs, bullets, bold, italics, "curly" quotes, or other special characters?

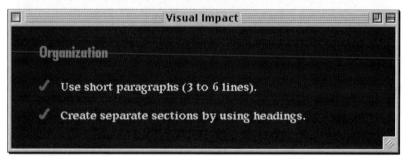

Visual Impact

Organization

✓ Use short paragraphs (3 to 6 lines).

✓ Create separate sections by using headings.

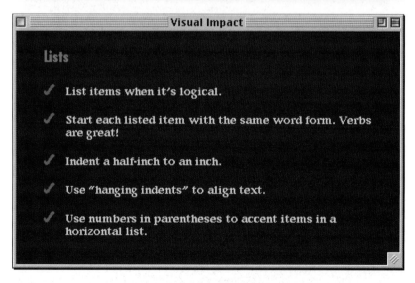

Visual Impact

Lists

✓ List items when it's logical.

✓ Start each listed item with the same word form. Verbs are great!

✓ Indent a half-inch to an inch.

✓ Use "hanging indents" to align text.

✓ Use numbers in parentheses to accent items in a horizontal list.

How do you want to be perceived by others?

> Efficient?
> Friendly?
> Business-like?
> Careful?
> Organized?

Your e-mail correspondence says a lot about you. When you pay attention to style, you will project the image you want.

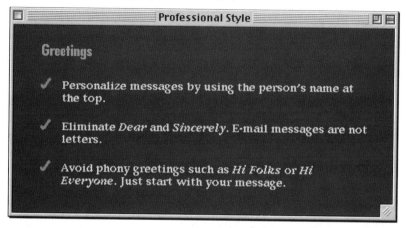

Professional Style

Greetings

✓ Personalize messages by using the person's name at the top.

✓ Eliminate *Dear* and *Sincerely*. E-mail messages are not letters.

✓ Avoid phony greetings such as *Hi Folks* or *Hi Everyone*. Just start with your message.

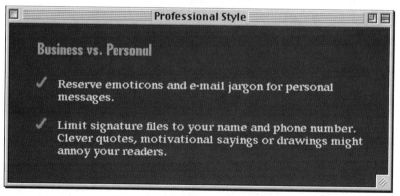

Professional Style

Business vs. Personal

✓ Reserve emoticons and e-mail jargon for personal messages.

✓ Limit signature files to your name and phone number. Clever quotes, motivational sayings or drawings might annoy your readers.

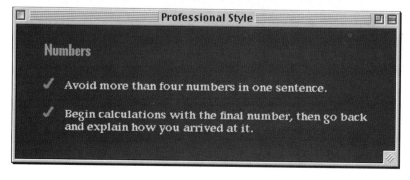

Professional Style

Numbers

✓ Avoid more than four numbers in one sentence.

✓ Begin calculations with the final number, then go back and explain how you arrived at it.

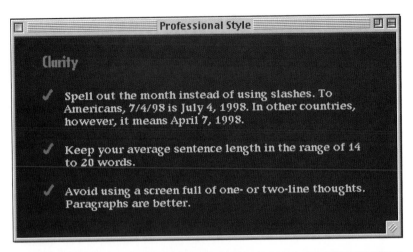

Clarity

✓ Spell out the month instead of using slashes. To Americans, 7/4/98 is July 4, 1998. In other countries, however, it means April 7, 1998.

✓ Keep your average sentence length in the range of 14 to 20 words.

✓ Avoid using a screen full of one- or two-line thoughts. Paragraphs are better.

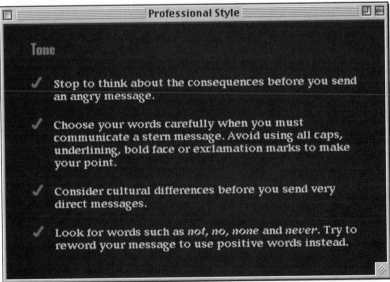

Tone

✓ Stop to think about the consequences before you send an angry message.

✓ Choose your words carefully when you must communicate a stern message. Avoid using all caps, underlining, bold face or exclamation marks to make your point.

✓ Consider cultural differences before you send very direct messages.

✓ Look for words such as *not, no, none* and *never.* Try to reword your message to use positive words instead.

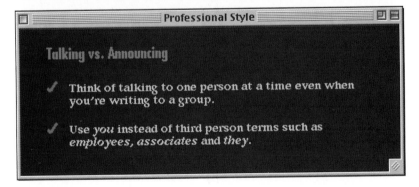

Talking vs. Announcing

✓ Think of talking to one person at a time even when you're writing to a group.

✓ Use *you* instead of third person terms such as *employees, associates* and *they.*

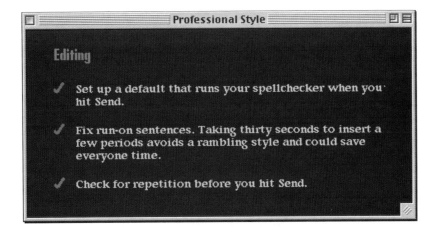

Professional Style

Editing

✓ Set up a default that runs your spellchecker when you hit Send.

✓ Fix run-on sentences. Taking thirty seconds to insert a few periods avoids a rambling style and could save everyone time.

✓ Check for repetition before you hit Send.

Business
Judgment

Reader
Focus

Visual
Impact

Professional
Style

E-mail
Success!

Simple Steps to E-mail Success

Business Writing Specialists since 1978

The Writing Exchange is a training and consulting firm headquartered in Chatham, New Jersey. Business writing is our specialty. Our services contribute to our clients' productivity, efficiency, quality and customer relations. *Fortune 500* companies throughout the United States and major international firms rely on us for seminars, private coaching and editing services.

Open Enrollment Seminars

We offer one-day open enrollment seminars that are limited in size to ensure individual attention. Call us at (973) 822-8400 for current dates, locations and registration details.

On-site Seminars

Over 70% of our course participants attend on-site programs. Unlike open enrollment seminars, these workshops allow clients to:

- Enjoy the convenience of scheduling the best time for everyone.
- Save on travel costs.
- Focus on only what is important for their organization.
- Discuss confidential issues that are inappropriate at an open enrollment seminar.
- Add another day of training and still keep the per person cost below our open enrollment registration fee.

Select The Write Start™ for a general audience or any of these tailored courses:

Bottom Line Financial Writing
E-mail Success
Grammar for Business
Proofreading Success
Selling on Paper
The Write Start for Auditors
The Write Start for Bankers
The Write Start for Engineers and Scientists
The Write Start for Support Staff
The Write Start for Systems Professionals
Writing and Editing for Managers

Coaching by Mail

Are your letters, memos, e-mail messages and reports taking you too long? Are they projecting the image you want to convey? Does your writing have power and impact? If you're not sure, get some feedback from a pro!

You don't have to attend a seminar or watch a videotape. Just send sample letters to us and let us design models and make suggestions specifically for you. Since your own writing is the central focus, you won't waste time on things you don't need.

How It Works

- Call (973) 822-8400 to enroll. We will send you a two-page Business Writing Audit to help you determine your own goals.

- Send us five pages of your unedited correspondence along with your completed Business Writing Audit. Your Writing Exchange coach will send you: (1) a letter highlighting your strengths, (2) detailed comments about each page—what's working and what's not, (3) new models based on your letters, and (4) a Personal Action Plan that offers specific direction.

- Try out the new techniques you've learned and send us three new pages of writing. Your coach will send you more feedback and ideas you can use.

Materials

In addition to the personalized coaching, you receive two books and a job aid:

- *Selling on Paper—The Way to Write to Customers*, a 125-page book that provides examples of letters to customers as well as internal memos and reports.

- *The Writing Exchange Business Style Guide*, a 233-page book that gives you straight answers to questions about grammar, usage and style.

- *Reminders from The Writing Exchange*, a 12-page pocket-size booklet that summarizes effective writing techniques.

The Writing Exchange Business Style Guide

Here's a book you can rely on for straight answers to questions about grammar, usage and style. The explanations are in plain English. The chapters are short, and the format is so appealing you will forget you're reading a book of rules. More than 750 business examples show you what's correct and what's not. You don't have to wade through stuffy explanations; you simply match the examples to your own questions.

The Writing Exchange Business Style Guide
A Concise, Practical Reference for Error-free Business Correspondence
ISBN 0-9643824-0-7; 233 pages, softcover, with comprehensive index
$21.95

Selling on Paper – The Way to Write to Customers

You don't have to be in a sales position to benefit from *Selling on Paper*. No matter what your title is, you're always "selling" when you put your ideas on paper. Although most of the examples are follow-up letters to external customers, the concepts apply to any business document—even to e-mail messages!

This is a seminar in a book. As you read, you'll find six checkpoints called *Your Editing Checklist*. You can use these to measure the customer focus of your documents. More than 30 effective and ineffective models make it easy for you to recognize the difference between merely acceptable correspondence and truly exceptional correspondence.

Selling on Paper
The Way to Write to Customers
ISBN 0-9643824-1-5; 125 pages, softcover, with index
$24.95

Reminders from The Writing Exchange

This handy 12-page pocket-size booklet summarizes effective writing techniques.

Here are two sample pages:

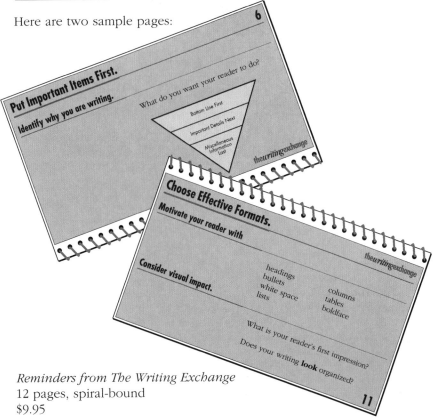

Reminders from The Writing Exchange
12 pages, spiral-bound
$9.95

Order Form

Fax or mail a copy of this page to:

WRIXpress
Division of The Writing Exchange, Inc.
466 Southern Boulevard
Chatham, New Jersey 07928
Telephone: (973) 822-8400 or (800) WRITE99 (974-8399)
Facsimile: (973) 822-8411
E-mail: WritingEx@aol.com

☐ *The Writing Exchange Business Style Guide*
  Quantity: _____ x $21.95* = _____

☐ *Simple Steps to E-mail Success*
  Quantity: _____ x $14.95* = _____

☐ *Reminders from The Writing Exchange*
  Quantity: _____ x $9.95* = _____

☐ *Selling on Paper*
  Quantity: _____ x $24.95* = _____

* To obtain information about quantity discounts for
  more than 10 copies, contact WRIXpress.

Total: _____

Sales Tax: _____
  Shipments to New Jersey only, add 6%.

Shipping and Handling: _____
  $6.00/first; $1.00/each additional.
  Reminders: $1.50/first; $.75/each additional.

Grand Total: _____
  We will send an invoice with your shipment.

Ship to: _____

_____

_____

_____

Bill to: _____

_____

_____

_____

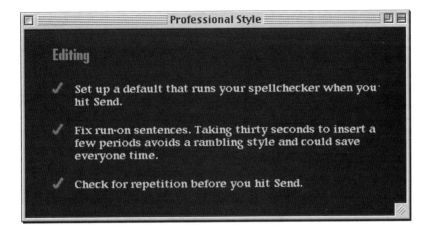

Editing

✓ Set up a default that runs your spellchecker when you hit Send.

✓ Fix run-on sentences. Taking thirty seconds to insert a few periods avoids a rambling style and could save everyone time.

✓ Check for repetition before you hit Send.

About the Author

Joy Van Skiver is president of The Writing Exchange, Chatham, New Jersey. She founded this training and consulting firm in 1978.

Thousands of professionals have learned how to write more effectively in Ms. Van Skiver's open enrollment seminars and workshops at corporations. She attributes her success to her realistic view of business writing. Her specialty is working with managers and executives, and with sales, marketing and technical professionals who must communicate the most important information in the least amount of time.

Ms. Van Skiver's other published works include:

> *Selling on Paper – The Way to Write to Customers*
>   WREXpress, 1997
> *The Writing Exchange Business Style Guide – A Concise,*
>   *Practical Reference for Error-free Business Correspondence*
>   WREXpress, 1995
> "Setting Up a Business Writing Program" in *The Human*
>   *Resources Employee Communications Guide*
>   Warren Gorham Lamont, 1992

She earned a bachelor's degree in English and Psychology at Houghton College, Houghton, New York, where she was honored with the Communications Excellence Award.

A member of the American Society for Training and Development, she has appeared as a guest speaker for professional organizations in advertising, training, healthcare and sales.

Colophon

Simple Steps to E-mail Success was produced on a Power Computing PowerTower Pro 225 Macintosh clone using Adobe PageMaker 6.52, Adobe Illustrator 8.0, Aldus FreeHand 4.0b, Microsoft Word 98, Microsoft Excel 98 and Microsoft Outlook Express 4.01.

Page proofs were made at 1200 dpi on a XANTÉ Accel-a-Writer 3DN, and final output was created at 2540 dpi on a Gerber platesetter using Harlequin Precision Screening.

Main type families are Garamond and Futura. Incidental typefaces are Avant Garde, Bauer Bodoni, Charcoal, Monaco and Zapf Dingbats.

Burton A. Spielman, WREXpress, designed and produced the book.

Quebecor Books, Kingsport, Tennessee, printed the book.